<u>Instru</u>

1) Have fun with this journal

2) Follow the instructions in whatever way you wish

3) The pages can be completed in any order you choose

4) Add colour with pens, crayons or paint

5) Don't let anyone else tell you what to do – it's YOUR journal

6) Enjoy yourself !!

Write your name in bubble letters:

_____

Where do you wish you lived?

_____

What's the Yummiest thing ever?

_____

Name someone you love:

_____

What's your most treasured thing?:

_____

Rip out this page and make a paper lantern

Stick

Fold

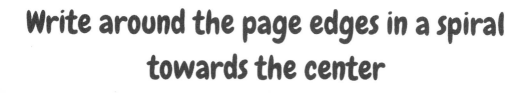

Write around the page edges in a spiral towards the center

Spend a week drawing a tree
Add more branches each day
For 7 days

Write a memory in each box
Cut the page along the lines
Fold each rectangle and
and place in a jar
Open the jar in a year
and read all the memories

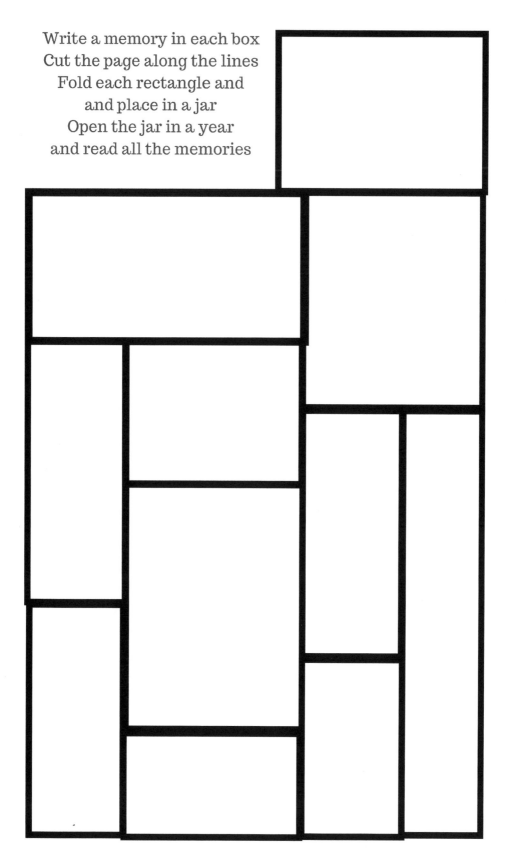

FINISH THE DOODLE

Cover the page with circles

SMEAR THE PAGE WITH ICE CREAM

Draw the longest line you can

Leave this page blank

Write a positive message here, tear out the page and leave it to be found

Tear into the tiniest of tiny pieces
hold in your hand &
throw into the air like confetti

Adorn this page with fingerprints

Trace around your bare toes

Go outside & use a magnifying glass and the sun to scorch this page (but don't set fire to the journal)

Free The Lines

Draw or Doodle whilst in a public place

Stamp on this page with muddy boots

Cut Two Eye Holes and Make a Mask

PLACE THE BOOK ON YOUR HEAD. NOW
DRAW A DINOSAUR WITHOUT LOOKING

Cover the page with SCRIBBLES

PAINT WITH YOUR FINGERS AND FRUIT JUICE

Step through the journal

+ | +

+ | +

+ | +

+ | +

+ | +

+ | +

+ | +

+ | +

+ | +

+ | +

+ | +

+ | +

Fold along the middle and cut the solid lines with scissors
Next cut from the EDGE of the page to the + sign

Write a comic book story

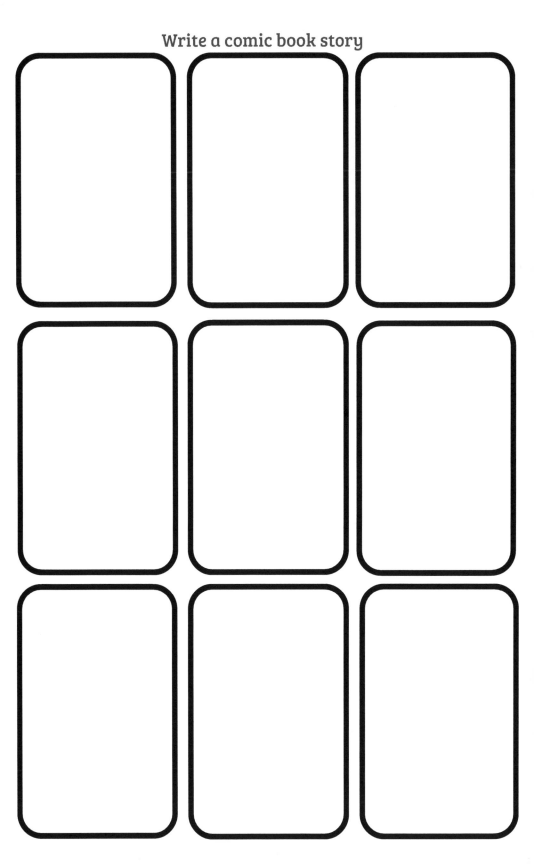

Glue in a feather

MAKE HOLES

Adorn this page with Coin Rubbings

JOIN THE DOTS

FILL THIS PAGE WITH HEARTS

Smash an egg here

Stick in 3 pieces of trash

Wave The
Book In
The Air
Like You
Just Don't
Care

Cut a slit in this page and post
something through it

Turn the Slit into a Doodle or Drawing

TEAR THIS PAGE OUT
SCRUMPLE INTO A BALL
THROW AS HIGH INTO THE AIR AS YOU CAN

PLACE THE BOOK ON THE FLOOR AND STAND ON THIS PAGE ON ONE LEG FOR 1 MINUTE

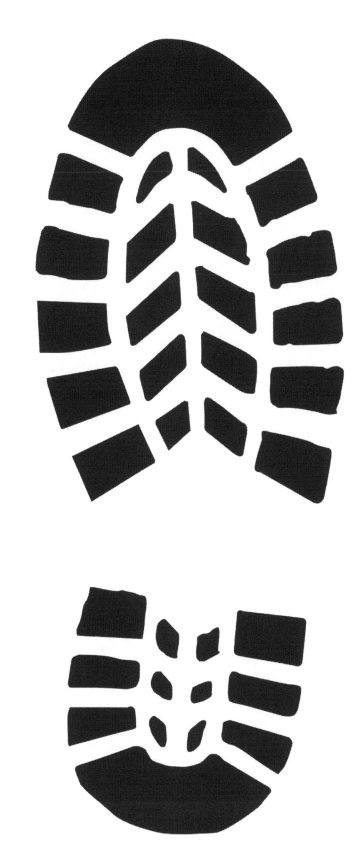

teLL mE a jOkE

Kiss this page 5 times

Gaze out of a window whilst you count to 100.

Write or draw what you saw.

I am THE BEST..........

COVER THIS PAGE WITH TRIANGLES

Rub shaving cream or whipped cream into this page

Cut out a photo of someone from a
newspaper or magazine.
Stick it here.
Graffiti on them eg devil horns, speech
bubble

Today, I am Grateful for

make a message by sticking in individual letters cut from a magazine or newspaper

STAND UP TALL AND SHOUT THE WORD

"Strong"

Trace around your hand

Use a cotton swab and lemon juice to write or draw.
Ask an adult to iron this page with a low heat

Chuck the
book
down
some
stairs

Tear out this page and use it to

wrap a small item.

Give it to someone else to unwrap

INVITE A FRIEND FOR A GAME OF DOTS

Rub or Spray this page to make it smell gorgeous

DRAW YOUR TREE INCLUDING ROOTS TO KEEP IT STRONG

Get this page dirty

Can you leave this page blank?

Tear out this page & tear into 4 pieces. Write a positive message on each piece. Leave each piece where someone else will find it.

Tear out this page
Make a paper aeroplane
Launch it into a public space
Leave for someone else to enjoy

tear out this page
cut along the lines
hang from the middle on a piece of
cotton thread or string

COVER THIS PAGE WITH STICKERS OF ANY KIND

Add some metal to this page

PAINT THIS PAGE WITH COFFEE

Paint your ear and make some prints

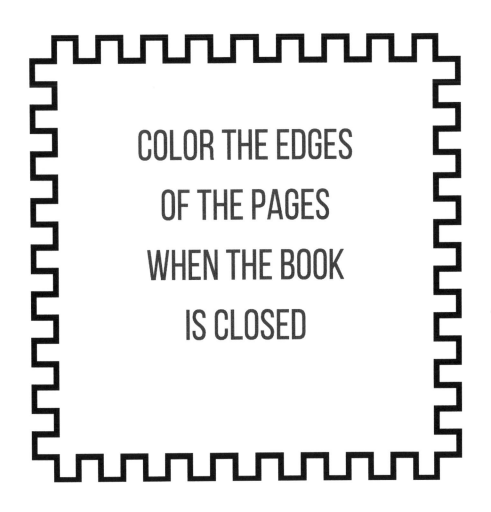

COLOR THE EDGES
OF THE PAGES
WHEN THE BOOK
IS CLOSED

Freeze
this
book
over
night

Tear out this page and fold over a cup. Secure with a rubber band. Tap out a rhythm with a pencil.

Smear With Berries

SPATTER WITH PAINT THEN CLOSE THE BOOK
STAND ON THE BOOK

Fill this page with Stars

Cut into strips.
Weave in strips of something else.

COLOUR OUTSIDE THE LINES

Cover this page with green things

GO BACK

and

number

the pages

This is YOUR page
Choose something you will enjoy

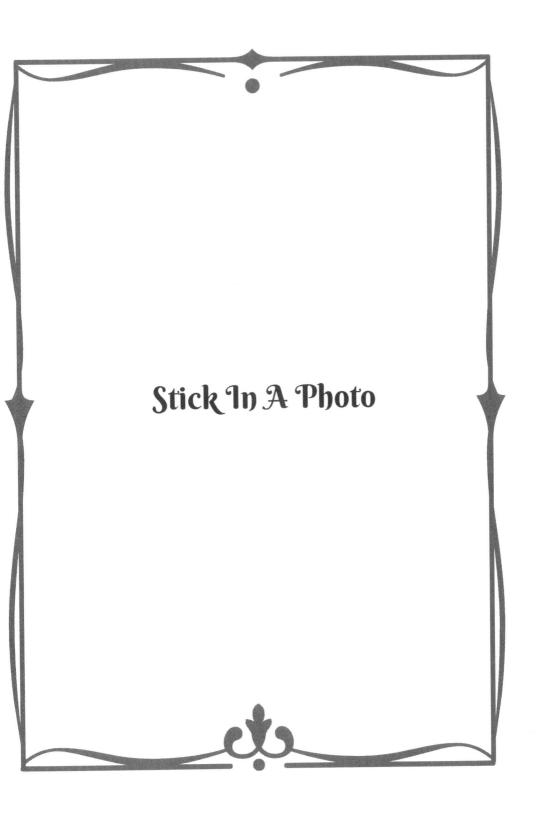

Stick In A Photo

Date Completed:

Made in the USA
San Bernardino, CA
19 March 2019